31 Days of Spiritual Wisdom
A Month in the Proverbs

Joel Dorman, D.Min.

To my love: my wife Patty who first led me to the Lord's wisdom in reading the Proverbs daily

CONTENTS

ACKNOWLEDGMENTS

There are men in my life most call "pastors." These same men bless me by allowing me to call them "friends." It is your wisdom manifested through me scattered throughout these pages.

FOREWORD

This little book started as a series of blog posts at my website "Life Meets Theology" (www.lifemeetstheology.com). It was the incredible, gracious people reading who encouraged me to turn this into a book. My hope is this small collection of thoughts based on one Proverb a day will help you grow deeper in your walk with Jesus.

This resource is not meant to replace your daily Bible study, but instead, is intended to serve as an alternative you can pursue for thirty days. The idea is for you to read a chapter of Proverbs every day and then turn to the pages of this book for a devotional thought on a few verses from that day's reading.

My prayer is that this little book helps you engage with the wisdom from Heaven as we move through this life on our journey home.

Joel Dorman

1 - A MANUAL FOR LIFE (PROVERBS 1:1-6)

Several years ago, the Lord drastically changed the direction of my life, and I still haven't recovered. ☺

I spent all of High School knowing what I was going to be. I loved music and anything related to it. The Lord whispered my name when I was fifteen and told me what I was supposed to be focusing on: becoming a pastor of music and worship. Sweet!

Through that first church in north Mississippi all the way to California, the Lord had me on a lot of adventures with music, worship, theology, and production.

Then, he whispered my name again. What I had prepared to be and was doing was now going to be laid aside. Now, I was going to begin focusing on teaching the Bible instead of singing the Bible. Now, if you don't know: there's a big difference between the two!

In making the transition, I wondered what in the world I would do with the musical, theatrical, and production experience I'd amassed in about seventeen years of worship ministry. Honestly, it felt almost like

I'd wasted that part of my life. Don't get me wrong: the ministry was fantastic, and I worked with some amazing world-changers but if I was now called to lay all that down…why in the world did I have to learn it in the first place?

The Lord drastically changed the direction of my life and although I'm still trying to stay "a retired worship pastor", the wisdom He taught me was proven immeasurable. God had a plan all along…who knew?

It took a few years for me to see God's ultimate purpose in this. It may take longer for you. Regardless, we find a significant reminder in Scripture about our need to gain wisdom from God's perspective. King Solomon, the son of King David, told us his purpose statement for writing what is called the book of Proverbs in **Proverbs 1:1-6**. Therein, we find the manual we need for understanding:

> *The proverbs of Solomon son of David, king of Israel: for gaining wisdom and instruction; for understanding words of insight; for receiving instruction in prudent behavior, doing what is right and just and fair; for giving prudence to those who are simple, knowledge and discretion to the young— let the wise listen and add to their learning, and let the discerning get guidance— for understanding proverbs and parables,*
> *the sayings and riddles of the wise.*

The wisdom we need to make sense out of the twists and turns in life doesn't come from mere age. It comes from saturating our minds and hearts in the Lord's wisdom. One reason I love reading the Proverbs so much is it will change your thinking in a hurry. When you realize how much "life" is packed into this thirty-one chapter book, you'll wonder where it's been your whole life.

Not only does it teach our minds to think like one of God's children, but it also trains our hearts to beat like one too. I encourage you to stay with this resource for this entire month.

Also, read an entire chapter of Proverbs every day. At the end of this month, not only will you have read through an entire book of the Bible, you'll find the Lord transforming your mind and heart as He instructs you in the manual for life.

2 – SHOPPING FOR SUCCESS
(PROVERBS 2:7-8)

What would you tell me to advise me to get to where you are?

I can safely say: I've never been asked this before. Ever. I mean EVER. Perhaps for a good reason, but I've never been asked this question before. Then this conversation with this young man happened, and I found myself trying to answer a question I'd never thought about.

I stumbled and stammered over my words for a few minutes while I prayed that profoundly spiritual prayer in my mind, "GOD, HELP!! NOW WOULD BE A GOOD TIME FOR SOME VERBATIM INSPIRATION!!!!!"

It didn't come, but I think—I hope—I managed to point this young man towards his Creator and His Son, our Savior, so he could discover why the Lord had given him a second chance at life.

The question was a fair one (and one I'm prepared for next time!) and certainly not one Scripture is silent over. The world is shopping for "success". And like someone heading to the grocery store without a list and on an empty stomach, we're not even sure what we're looking for and often end up simply eating "junk" because it satisfies that need to feel "successful".

And then we read passages like **Proverbs 2:7-8**:

He holds success in store for the upright,
he is a shield to those whose walk is blameless,
for he guards the course of the just
and protects the way of his faithful ones.

We can turn to the Proverbs for great counsel for a great many things. One key to understanding the Proverbs, however, is to make sure we're using words the same way. We can read this Proverb and think *"success"* is monetary or positional. But we'd be wrong.

In Hebrew (the original language of most of the Old Testament), *"success"* is not synonymous with *"make you wealthy, highly respected, or well known."* Instead, the concept is more like possession of a particular type of wisdom that grants you soundness or efficiency.

Think of it this way: the Hebrew idea of "success" is one of competence to live life well.

So in context, the author of Proverbs tells us the location of this type of competence to live life well: the Lord. It is the Lord who stores up success for us. It is the Lord who *"is a shield to those whose walk is blameless."* It is the Lord Who *"guards the course of the just and protects the way of the faithful ones."*

When our wisdom leads us to the competence to live this life well, we stop shopping for success in those things that are temporary. We focus on the eternal. After all, *"The fear of the Lord is the beginning of wisdom, and knowledge of the Holy One is understanding"* (**Proverbs 9:10**).

We're not going to find our Savior's definition of success until we find Him in submission and humility. For it is in *that* place where we can realize the embrace of Jesus as He described it in **John 10:27–30**.

"My sheep listen to my voice; I know them, and they follow me. I give them eternal life, and they shall never perish; no one will snatch them out of my hand. My Father, who has given them to me, is greater than all; no one can snatch them out of my Father's hand. I and the Father are one."

Where do I need to be to find worth? In the embrace of a Savior that knows me better than I know myself and yet loves me anyway.

Dearly beloved of the Lord, stop shopping for success where this world tells you and start buying droves of stock in the limitless supply of the Lord's gift at competence to live life well.

3 – RUN TO YOUR KNEES! (PROVERBS 3:5-6)

"Trust in yourself, and you are doomed to disappointment; trust in your friends, and they will die and leave you; trust in reputation, and some slanderous tongue may blast it; but trust in God, and you are never to be confounded in time or eternity."

19th Century American Evangelist Dwight Moody

Great advice. But not original to the famous preacher of the Gospel. It's an expansion of two verses tucked neatly into the book of Proverbs. If you're like me, you've probably heard **Proverbs 3:5-6** a lot.

Trust in the Lord with all your heart
and lean not on your own understanding;
in all your ways submit to him,
and he will make your paths straight.

But maybe you're newer to faith, and you haven't heard it as much. If that's you, I'm honored to show you a real gem in the Proverbs!

This first command, *"trust in the Lord with all your heart,"* could also be expressed as *"run for refuge to Yahveh."* It seems one of the hardest things to do as a Christian is to trust the Lord NO MATTER WHAT. Yet, the wisdom of Solomon through the Holy Spirit tells us to run **to** the Lord when we face problems and not run **away**.

When trouble comes, what's our instinct? Run away. But what are we supposed to do? Run to.

Our own knowledge is based on limited experience and our own sinfulness and "blind spots." The Lord, on the other hand, sees all and is fully aware of the circumstances, permutations, possibilities, and outcome. Logically, who would you trust?

Flowing from that understanding is a willingness to submit to the Lord in all things. After all, He really does know best, and so we can trust Him. Even when things don't make sense, we can trust Him.

And how do we learn about Him? Experience is certainly one way, but experience is very limited and highly subjective. The best way? Reading and interacting with His word. It's often said, *"when we know the Word of God better, we will better know the God of the Word."* Well put!

So the next time you face adversity or a trial, don't run away—that's using your limited experience. Instead, run to your knees. Read the Word. Hear His voice. Don't lean on your experience. Lean on His.

4 – WATCHING YOUR STEP
(PROVERBS 4:18-19)

Don't be surprised when the world acts like the world.

I don't remember where or when I heard this great jewel of truth, but it stuck with me and resonates in my head every time I watch or read the news. There are times when I think, *"Reason has apparently escaped us as a society."*

And apart from Christ, reason indeed has left us. Apart from Christ, it's not ever there in the first place. We as Christians can be shocked by how far people will sink into immorality, and we shake our heads in disbelief. At the same time, however, we must remember we can't be surprised when the world acts like the world. They don't know any better.

This is the principle found in **Proverbs 4:18-19**:

The path of the righteous is like the morning sun,
shining ever brighter till the full light of day.
But the way of the wicked is like deep darkness;
they do not know what makes them stumble.

As disciples of the Master, we should know better than to stumble into the ditch. After all, the Holy Spirit illuminates our path. But apart from this illumination and guidance, our families, friends, and coworkers are left to grope through the treacherous waters of this world while sprinting at full speed. No wonder they run into "stuff."

Today's Scripture passage reminds us *they do not know what makes them stumble.* It's like they're so close to the problem they can't see it. After all, we are the problem. Not we as Christians, but we as humans. It is our sin keeping us in darkness. It is our dirtiness keeping our eyes mired to the dangers all around us.

And apart from the grace of God the Father through Jesus Christ, we Christians would still be running full speed into the train of death heading straight for us.

But, thank the Lord, His love has shone into our dark hearts and burned away the sin and shame and gave us life and freedom. *"I am the light of the world,"* Jesus said in **John 8:12**, *"Whoever follows me will never walk in darkness, but will have the light of life."*

Our charge now is to reflect the mercy of God given to us into the lives of those around us. At the same time, we must lovingly remain patient as they continue acting like we once did.

As we watch our step, we have to remember to not blame the world for acting like the world. Until we show them *"the most excellent way"* (**1 Corinthians 12:31b**), they won't know any better. And even then, we're not their Savior.

Watch your step and step towards those who are stepping through darkness to lead them to His light.

5 – DISCERNING THE FERTILIZERS (PROVERBS 5:1-2)

"I just don't love her anymore."

As a pastor, I've heard these sad words off the lips of more men than I can recall. Face after face, relationship after relationship suffers at the hands of this game of emotions.

My first response (once the guy's done talking) is usually the Tina Turner song title: *"What's love got to do with it?"*

While I certainly don't mean the concept of the song, I often talk about the utter worthlessness of the statement of *"I don't love her."* Often what's happened is a lack of good fertilizer in the mind and heart of those men that has resulted in a dying *"yard."*

My counsel often further comes at the wisdom of **Proverbs 5**, which opens in **verses 1 and 2** with this:

My son, pay attention to my wisdom,
turn your ear to my words of insight,
that you may maintain discretion
and your lips may preserve knowledge.

These opening phrases begin a lengthy section about marital faithfulness. Yet, here in these verses, we find no direct mention of marriage. Strange for an introduction, huh?

Or is it...

There's a powerful warning embedded in these little verses. We're cautioned to listen carefully to the ears of our teacher so we can maintain *"discretion."* We hear this word, and we immediately think of issues of privacy or being *"discreet."* We might even think this verse is talking about modesty. But it isn't.

In Hebrew (the original language of most of the Old Testament), the word translated *"discretion"* refers to our ability to discern truth from error—right from wrong. At the least, it relates to our consciences, but at its heart, this word refers to our heart's ability to maintain synchronization with the Lord's commandments and wisdom for a blessed life.

The beginning of our ability to have a healthy relationship of any sort—and certainly a marriage, is our Biblically empowered *"discretion."* As disciples of Jesus, we need to cultivate the ability to know right from wrong in all circumstances when it comes to our marriages.

And this *"discretion"*—this ability to know the truth from a lie also is accompanied by the desire that our *"lips may preserve knowledge."* When we embrace the Biblical definition of right and wrong, wise and foolish, beneficial and harmful, our lifestyles reflect it. How many times have we been tempted (in any number of circumstances) with the lie of "the grass is greener on the other side"?

But it isn't. It just has different fertilizer.

When we are Biblically discreet and our mouths—even our lifestyles—reflect the knowledge of the Bible's commands for righteous, healthy, good, whole, and blessed living, our primary human relationship (our marriage) is the model of it.

The reason this section of Proverbs opens its discussion about marital faithfulness is because adultery doesn't begin with our bodies. Read this slowly: adultery always starts with our minds.

Feed your mind with Biblical-based fertilizer. Let your life be a model of this saturation. And watch the fruit of your marriage begin to reflect the life Jesus has given you.

6 – FAILING TO PLAN (PROVERBS 6:6-8)

"To fail to plan is to plan to fail"

And I think most people with a brain will nod and agree. But what do we do with it? How do we plan in such a way so we *don't* fail? Now <u>that</u> would be helpful, right?

We read in **Proverbs 6:6-8**:

Go to the ant, you sluggard;
consider its ways and be wise!
It has no commander,
no overseer or ruler,
yet it stores its provisions in summer
and gathers its food at harvest.

This Proverb isn't difficult to understand. Without a commanding officer or any kind of supervisor, the Creator endows an ant with the ability to plan. It gathers provisions in summer and food at harvest time. Ants are ready for winter. They're not surprised. And they don't have a calendar.

We do.

Why are we unprepared for the expense of the Christmas season?

Why are we unprepared for the expense of birthdays? Why are we unprepared to give to our church or those in need?

We fail to plan and therefore, plan to fail. But this is more than just a Proverb about saving money—although that's certainly a valid application. The concept is far bigger with further reaching implications. This Proverb is teaching us about responsibility.

Personal responsibility. An ant takes personal responsibility and does its part in preparing the entire colony for those seasons when there will not be a lot of resources. Why don't we?

Unfortunately, I think the same thing making us unique is also what can cripple us. Intuition. We presume on the future. We live for today. We ignore the cycle of the past.

And just like the cost of Christmases, birthdays, and giving: we fail to plan on the recurring nature of life. We fail to take personal responsibility and in the process let our "colony" down.

This is the message and warning of **Proverbs 6:6-8**. We must be on guard. Learn our lessons. Take responsibility. And plan. Then, we will plan to succeed and will better ride out the ebb and flow of financial life.

7 – CHOOSE "NAVIGATE" (PROVERBS 7:1-4)

I'm directionally challenged.

That confession isn't new, and it's certainly been the subject of a lot of my blogs and message illustrations. But the issue for me isn't just embracing the fact that I'm a shame to my gender because I can't find my way back to or from anywhere. The issue for me is learning to deal with my "handicap."

My solution? Google Maps on my iPhone. No, this isn't a commercial for either one of those products; it's an admission to my solution. I keep GPS very close at my side—literally: my phone rests in a holster on my side. If I need to get to the grocery store: recall that location in my maps program. Get to the movie theater from my office? No problem after a few touches on the responsive screen of my smartphone.

I would be up poop creek without a paddle if my GPS ever stopped working. I'd be lost and scared.

Did you know our spiritual lives have similar guiding devices built into them? **Proverbs 7:1-4** reminds us…

My son, keep my words and store up my commands within you. Keep my commands and you will live; guard my teachings as the apple of your eye. Bind them on your fingers; write them on the tablet of your heart. Say to wisdom, "You are my sister," and to insight, "You are my relative."

In the context of **Proverbs 7**, these four verses are an introduction to applying wisdom in avoiding adulterous women. However, this introduction gives us a stark warning to the necessity of our guiding devices for our spiritual formation.

We are commanded to *"keep…store…guard…bind…write"* the wisdom of the Lord into our existence. I doubt there are many Christians reading this who will argue with this. The issue is this: since we know this is something we should do, why aren't we doing it?

Why don't we *"keep…store…guard…bind…write"* the wisdom of the Lord into our existence? Why do we bounce around like a pinball through life, banging against pain after pain all the while ignoring the lessons our Heavenly Father is trying to teach us? If we know what we should do and refuse to do it, what does that make us?

Stubborn? Definitely. Defiant? Yep. Stupid? That too.

For us to have the manual for living (that would be the Bible combined with prayer and worship) readily available to us and to ignore what it teaches is just dumb. No wonder we keep having to go through the same trials and troubles over and over! The Lord is trying to teach us what we don't want to teach ourselves.

It's like me complaining about Google or Apple if I don't type in the address and click "Navigate". It's not their fault if I'm too stubborn, defiant, or stupid to use the tool I need. Let me get lost for a few hours and I might figure out the route. Or I can use the tool, type the address, click "Navigate" and be there in seven minutes.

So what's it gonna be, follower of Christ? Are you going to dig into the Word of the Lord this year, coupling it with prayer and worship? Are you going to sharpen your use of the spiritual tools of faith this year?

I hope so…otherwise, it's gonna be an extra long, extra painful, and extra twisting pathway.

Instead, I urge you to open your Bible, heart, and mind and "click Navigate."

8 – DECISIONS, DECISIONS
(PROVERBS 8:35-36)

"Just make up your mind already!"

Surely we can all identify with that sentiment. How many times have we found ourselves in situations as a spouse, friend, colleague, or observer and just wanted to scream, "Just make up your mind already!"? I have.

In our lives with Christ, we will find ourselves in similar situations: we will have a choice to make. Choose one path, and we are blessed. Choose the other, and we will find only problems. When we hit the "fork in the road," the path we choose will set the course for our lives from then onward.

Proverbs 8:35-36 instructs:

For those who find me find life
and receive favor from the Lord.
But those who fail to find me harm themselves;
all who hate me love death."

The choice is striking. First, there's this: seek God, find favor. As the Lord reminds us in **Jeremiah 29:13**, *"You will seek me and find me* *when you seek me with all your heart."* He wants to be found. The Lord isn't hiding out camouflaged in the underbrush of our lives trying to hide from us. Dear Christian, He's not sitting in a corner snickering at you in some kind of cruel game of hide and seek. Oh no. He's waiting to be found. Better than that, He's searching for us! Look at **Luke 15:11-32**.

Alternatively, if we fail to seek him, we shouldn't be surprised when we find harm. There is no option for "maybe". To make a choice against seeking God is to choose against Him. Do you live like a "functional atheist"? What I mean is this: do you confess Jesus as Lord but live as if there's no God? I don't mean you're a pagan or anything, but does harm come on you for the simple reason that you try to do it your way instead of God's way?

Your loving Savior still looks at you and says, *"But seek first his kingdom and his righteousness, and all these things will be given to you as well"* (**Matthew 6:33**).

Seek Him: you find life and protection.
Refuse to seek Him: you find harm and death.

So…just make up your mind already.

9 – READ THE INSTRUCTIONS!
(PROVERBS 9:10-12)

"I'll figure it out!"

How many men have spoken just these types of words when faced with a project whose completion might actually result in reaching for an instruction manual? It's the kind of thing we men seldom admit, but there are actually times "I'll figure it out" is a prelude to the complete and total rendering of said device or project as useless and hopelessly broken.

But how often we—men *and* women—attempt to go through life the same way: figuring it out without consulting the instruction manual. Instructions? Who needs instructions, right?

We read in **Proverbs 9:10-12**:

The fear of the Lord is the beginning of wisdom,
and knowledge of the Holy One is understanding.
For through wisdom your days will be many,
and years will be added to your life.
If you are wise, your wisdom will reward you;
if you are a mocker, you alone will suffer.

This is why I love the Proverbs: they are straightforward and undeniable. When we go through our lives as believers in Christ without consulting the manual, we are performing a prelude to the complete and total rendering of our lives as useless for the ultimate cause of the Kingdom.

We don't have to grope through the darkness trying to figure it out. God has shown us how to live. He has illuminated the path of blessing. Our realization of Who He is will be the foundation of our wisdom. Our comprehension of the storms of this life is an intimate awareness of our Lord.

As Christ continues to remake us into His image, we draw on His wisdom and understanding, so the world doesn't see us as bumbling idiots, but as those possessing, and having access to, the wisdom of God.

Jesus sends us "...*out like sheep among wolves. Therefore be as shrewd as snakes and as innocent as doves*" (**Matthew 10:16**).

10 – WEALTHY HANDS (PROVERBS 10:4)

I've yet to see a rich lazy person (that didn't inherit their money).

Have you? Looking through the Forbes list of billionaires (http://www.forbes.com/billionaires/list/#tab:overall), I noticed something while checking them out: they are all incredibly busy. They don't *"let the grass grow under their feet."* They are industrious and diligent. Hardworking and engaged. They are typically involved in multiple endeavors including charity work.

Interesting.

One adjective you would NOT use to describe this group is this: lazy. These aren't people sleeping in until noon every day and only working for a couple of hours.

While I don't wish to debate the morality of how these billionaires made their fortunes (I honestly don't know for the vast majority of them anyway), there is a lot we can learn from them.

And these hard-working qualities are something that a Biblical billionaire noticed too. He wrote in **Proverbs 10:4**:

Lazy hands make for poverty, but diligent hands bring wealth.

Written by King Solomon in the 10th century B.C., the Biblical billionaire observed that laziness only produces poverty. Now, before any of you think the Bible is saying if you're poor you're lazy, think again. The King is making an observation here that lazy hands are only capable of producing poverty while hard-working hands bring wealth.

There are a couple of keys in this passage. First are the words *"lazy hands"*. By this, Solomon is referring to the sloppy and shoddy work these hands produce. Lazy people don't work hard or diligently. They do the bare minimum (if that much!) and "clock out" as soon as they can (if not early). With that in mind, we would look at this proverb and think, *"Of course, shoddy and sloppy work will not be rewarded."*

Also, there's a lot of interpretive room for the word *"wealth"*. What is wealth? King Solomon could have written *"riches"*, but he wrote *"wealth"*. In a sense, he certainly means money, but there's a greater sense as well. It's referring to a growing financial stability. I know people who make very little money, yet have tremendous financial stability. These people are *"diligent"*.

At the same time, I've also known those making over six-figure salaries and are always broke and looking for more money. That's not wealth in the Biblical sense; that's not a growing financial stability.

In sum, the Holy Spirit through the ink and quill of the Biblical billionaire, King Solomon, is instructing us that steady, consistent, careful, self-starting work will be rewarded with growing financial stability while those who practice sloppy, shoddy, careless, inconsistent, and unmotivated work will receive shrinking financial stability.

The lesson of this Proverb: work not only harder but also smarter. Be diligent in what you do because if you're a Christian, you are not really working for humans. Our employer is the Lord (cf. **Colossians 3:23-24**).

11 – A TONGUE TO SINK A SHIP
(PROVERBS 11:13)

"Loose lips sink ships."

I remember where I was when I first heard that and it was told to me as a warning. A warning, in retrospect, that proved unneeded. However, this wise man was telling me a powerful truth. People with loose lips will sink the mightiest of ships. It doesn't matter who you are; you could say the wrong thing to the wrong person and end up being wrecked because of it.

King Solomon of Israel said the same thing as my friend, albeit more poetically in **Proverbs 11:13**:

A gossip betrays a confidence,
but a trustworthy person keeps a secret.

There are times we get ourselves into trouble because people find out something we did that we shouldn't have been doing. It's hard to have sympathy when that happens. But what about when someone just blabs your life across the megaphone of their world and freely shares your information with others? Why do they do that?

Because by their nature, they are gossips. As wise Solomon said:

they will betray our confidence. We shouldn't be surprised when they betray our private moments with them because they have a character flaw in them preventing them from keeping their mouths shut.

A trustworthy person, on the other hand, is someone who can keep a secret. They don't feel the compulsion to tell everyone everything they know. In humility, they guard your fears, insecurities, doubts, and struggles from the world wishing to tear you apart.

And therein is the crucial difference between a trustworthy person and a gossip: their pride. Have you heard the expression "knowledge is power"? What does a gossip have a lot of? Knowledge (whether it's true or not is another story!). Since they have a lot of knowledge about people, what do they have over them and over those without this knowledge? Yep! Power.

Gossips betray our confidence because it brings them power to share the "exclusive" knowledge they have. Many times, their retelling of your tales has less to do with you and more to do with them. You are, unfortunately, collateral damage on their way "to the top."

But those people who are humble before the Lord are trustworthy with even the "juiciest" of tidbits. They have no desire to hoard power and show it to others. Instead, they desire to help. After all, it's why they're listening to you in the first place.

Pray for the discernment and wisdom to quickly identify the difference between gossips and trustworthy people.

It'll save your ship.

12 – SPEECH SPEAKS (PROVERBS 12:23)

The first time I heard the term I literally LOL'd!

It was in the context of a workshop designed to help churches know how to find good small group leaders. For those who don't know, that's not as easy as it sounds. Among the great deep, thought-provoking tips and ideas, this one term stuck out to me.

Perhaps it was because of the context: we were instructed that these were not good small group leaders. So as someone who was involved with finding small group leaders, it really mattered that I didn't get sub-par ones.

We were told (and here's the term) to avoid "hyper-spiritual God talkers".[1]

Yep. Hyper-spiritual God talkers. And the reason I laughed out loud—and the reason you are too—is because we know exactly what that term means.

They're the ones who, whether well-meaning or not, always have a

---

[1] The author gratefully acknowledges Larry Osborne and his book *Sticky Church* for this great term and description.

Bible verse or a Christian platitude to offer to each and every situation they face. They seem to be very spiritual, and certainly, they seem very…um…zealous for God. Extremely dedicated and typically patronizing, they seem to have it all together and usually wonder why you don't.

Yeah.

Proverbs 12:23, however, offers this counsel to the hyper-spiritual God talker in all of us Christians:

The prudent keep their knowledge to themselves,
but a fool's heart blurts out folly.

Have you ever noticed those who are truly wise don't have to tell you? Don't you just <u>know</u> they're wise? After all, that's why you go to them in the first place. You know they're not fake. You know they're going to listen. And you know they're probably right.

But when we as Christians allow ourselves to travel down the path of legalistic, hyper-spiritual God talking, we start trying to interject how "wise" we are. But when we do this…if we're honest, we're interjecting our spiritual opinions because we just want to be right, noticed, esteemed, or regarded. We'll mask it as Christianity, but we're really just playing devil's advocate.

Please remember this: the way we speak will determine how others speak of us. If we're truly Biblically wise, then we won't have to tell people. They'll know. And we won't care if they know or not.

The only people the hyper-spiritual God talkers help are themselves. Let us strive to have the speech of others about us be words telling of wisdom, grace, and love.

13 – PRIDE AND PEACE (PROVERBS 13:10)

Do you want to be "right" or happy?

It's the beginning of a great a joke and drips with sarcasm, but there could be some truth for us to consider.

How much do we want to "win"?
How badly do we desire to be proven right in an argument?
Are we willing to take our passions and shove them down everyone else's throats—no matter what?

Or can we let some things go?

Many times, "right" is a philosophical perspective. Don't get me wrong: I'm NOT saying right and wrong are arbitrary categories because Scripture has defined morality and settled those issues.

I've just learned over the years we tend to fight over philosophy and not these "hard and fast" categories of morally right and wrong.

King Solomon of Israel seemed to notice this as well and wrote in **Proverbs 13:10**:

Where there is strife, there is pride,
but wisdom is found in those who take advice.

Someone who is wise will receive wisdom from someone else. It's interesting: wise people are wise because they listen to wise people.

Conversely, when our desire to be "right" overrides everything else, we'll fight, scratch, claw, demand, stomp, and snort over it.

Scripture calls this what it is: pride.

I've done my fair share of counseling as a pastor. After a few years of being frustrated by the constant returning and asking for the same counsel on the same issues, I changed my tactics. I started asking them a question: will you actually *try* to do the things I'm counseling you to do?

As we grow in wisdom, we learn to heed the counsel of others. We realize that we don't have all the answers and perhaps others can see our situations with greater clarity than we can.

What we find in Proverbs 13:10 is a challenge on our desires. Do we want to be "right" all the time or do we want to be content? Which is more important: peace or pride? See what I mean? It's a question of desire. It's testing our motivations.

Let's test our motivations right now in an area where we're experiencing strife. Are we truly morally and ethically right, or is just a matter of taste and we're just fighting to prove our "rightness"?

What's more valuable to you in your heart: being "right" or being happy?

14 – LOUD CONVERSATIONS
(PROVERBS 14:3)

It's amazing the conversations you have when your office is coffee shops.

Periodically, I make a rotation through various local coffee shops. And what you can talk about with people is astounding.

Eventually, you start to see patterns emerge:

- The fighter: He or she will always take the other side of the conversation just to watch the sparks fly.
- The peacekeeper: Just trying to keep everyone happy.
- The partier: Let's just have fun!
- The sage: When they speak, everyone listens.
- The fool: You wonder if they speak simply because they can't stand the silence. And they're always right (even if "the sage" has already spoken).

These aren't new patterns, of course. And I'm certainly not the first to notice them. I'm not even using the cleverest words, but it's remarkable how wisdom and folly replay themselves over and over in our conversations.

Proverbs 14:3 observes:

A fool's mouth lashes out with pride,
but the lips of the wise protect them.

Isn't it interesting that it's our words this Proverb focuses on? It's our words, after all, revealing what's happening in our hearts. Therefore, it's more than just words. The *"mouth"* and *"lips"* this Proverb refers to is a way of describing our behavior—our lives.

Simply put, there's a reason wise people are generally better off than the unwise. It's not just that they've amassed enough information to make informed decisions. Instead, there's a character that the Lord has developed in them producing a wise life. More than words—it's words put into action.

I want you to understand exactly what this Proverb is teaching. The expression *"lashes out with pride"* can also be conveyed as *"becomes a rod that beats him"* (New Living Translation).

The *"fool's mouth"* ends up bringing calamity on themselves. Through their words put into action, they prove they are without knowledge and—according to the Scriptures' use of the word—without the influence of God in their lives.

Oh dear one in Christ, evaluate your words because they reveal your heart. Evaluate your heart because it is demonstrated in your life. And your life is the "loud conversation" your friends, family, coworkers, and others are hearing.

15 – HYPER VERSUS HYPO EMOTIONALISM (PROVERBS 15:1)

"Oh no you didn't!"

This expression is typically the start of something ending in something stupid. Even if we've not said it, we've thought it when someone has said something to us that was definitely "across the line".

It wasn't that long ago that situation happened to me. A man accused me of using my influence as a pastor to lead the church down a heretical path. And let's just say he used "inflammatory language". I remember feeling my heart rate increase and my adrenaline kick in. In my sinful heart rose the words in my head, "Oh no you didn't just say that!"

Instead of dialogue, this man was only concerned with being right, yelling, and out-smarting me. Regardless of what I said to him next, he had already beaten me 100 times over in his head. What was I going to do? What was I going to say? The next words out of my mouth would define me in his eyes—after all, I was already a "heretic". At this point, the only thing left to do is assess my character.

What do you do in those moments when that "zinger" is right on the tip of your tongue, and the person across from you really deserves to be put back in their place?

We remember the wisdom of Solomon in **Proverbs 15:1**:

A gentle answer turns away wrath,
but a harsh word stirs up anger.

What?!?! You mean that's in the Bible?! I know. I was just as surprised as you. After all, idiots deserve to be whipped into their holes, right? You have the right to defend yourself, right?

A music theory professor (of all people) once gave a great paraphrase of this Proverb: *"never answer an emotionally charged comment with an emotionally charged comment."* It's stayed with me as much as this Proverb has. And has saved me many verbal fights because of it.

When we respond to someone with a gentle word, we defuse the situation. After all, when someone comes at you with all their emotions raging, they are looking for a fight. They are packed and ready to unload on you. If you give in to what your heart tells you to do, you'll swing back at their verbal assault, and you won't win. They will. And your testimony before the world will be tarnished.

But here's where reality sets in. In all likelihood, your gentle answer will only make them angrier. Yes. You read that right. My experience is that a gentle answer will increase their anger. But why? Because they came looking for a fight but you're not fighting.

Their anger will escalate, and they will sink lower.

You take the high road and deflect their wrath with a soft, slow tone.

They will then get personal and attack your character (if they weren't already!).

You take the high road and treat them with respect.

Easy?

34

Absolutely, positively, and completely NO.

A wise thing to do? The Christ-like thing to do? Absolutely, positively, and completely YES.

When you feel your blood pressure rising, and you feel the need to verbally attack back, take a deep breath, lower your volume, soften your tone, and ask them to talk to you when they're less emotional.

It'll save you the character-crushing embarrassment of sinking to their level and might actually demonstrate to them how a Christ-follower practices the spiritual discipline of self-control.

16 – THE WORST ADVICE I'VE EVER GOTTEN (PROVERBS 16:2)

"Just follow your heart."

I was in college, and she was still back home. We were obviously not going to get married. In my struggle, a well-meaning Christian brother observed my heartache and distress with my decision: break it off or try to maintain a long distance relationship.

It's critical to note here: this was **pre-social media days**. If we were to communicate, it would be through letters (mailed) or long-distance phone calls (where you pay by the minute). And I was four hours away. And my parents no longer lived in that city.

I took this friend's advice, and the results were disastrous.

But it's not the results I want to focus on. It's the disastrous counsel he gave: just follow your heart. We may say it differently, but at the end of the day, most are saying the same thing: trust your heart.

There is, however, a fatal flaw in this advice. Our hearts aren't impartial. They're always biased in our favor. As **Proverbs 16:2** states:

All a person's ways seem pure to them,

but motives are weighed by the Lord.

It doesn't matter the situation; we will end up being totally justified in our hearts. It won't take us long to justify anger, bitterness, revenge, depression, self-centeredness, cruelty, or any other feeling we desperately believe we *deserve* to feel.

And no wonder we see ourselves as right all the time: our ways *"seem pure to"* us.

The Lord, however, is an impartial judge and measures the motives of our hearts with perfectly balanced scales. His heart is pure; our hearts are deceptive. His heart is impartial; our hearts are always biased. His heart is holy; our hearts are hole-y. :-)

"What causes fights and quarrels among you?" **James** writes in **4:1–3**, *"Don't they come from your desires that battle within you? You desire but do not have, so you kill. You covet but you cannot get what you want, so you quarrel and fight. You do not have because you do not ask God. When you ask, you do not receive, because you ask with wrong motives, that you may spend what you get on your pleasures."*

In other words: most of our pain is self-induced. Why? We follow my well-intentioned friend's advice: follow your heart.

My advice, based on Scripture: **don't** follow your heart. It will lie to you.

Instead, learn to trust the heart of our Lord. Here are some takeaways:
1. Read Scripture daily. I suggest at least a chapter of Proverbs a day.
2. Pray daily. It's okay to confess your lack of discernment to the One who already knows it.
3. Submit daily. Realizing your heart will justify you in your own eyes, get used to submitting to the way that seems counter to what you're feeling. Even submitting doesn't feel "right" sometimes.

And—please—whatever you do, don't ever (ever!) tell someone to "follow their heart". Unless, of course, you want disaster to fall on them. In which case, you have other problems.

17 – RIGHT AND LONELY (PROVERBS 17:19)

You can be right and wrong at the same time.

And for those of us who are a little more "hard-nosed" push back against that statement with our typical scowl. If we're right, we're not wrong. But we can actually be "correct" in a statement or position and handle it completely wrong.

For all of us, there are moments when it happens. In those moments, we would be wise to remember **Proverbs 17:19**:

Whoever loves a quarrel loves sin;
whoever builds a high gate invites destruction.

I hope you're not one of those people that has to be right at all costs. But I'm sure you know them. They are a real drag to be around. It doesn't matter how small the issue is; they will be right—even if they're not! Scripture teaches us this kind of attitude is sin.

Understandably so: it's based on pride. It's our pride wanting to make sure we're right and wanting everyone else to know about it.

These kinds of people also have something else distinguishing them: they are isolated. This is what the Proverb means by they build *"a high gate."* Their arrogance and attitude of willingness to start a fight separate them from anyone who could speak truth in their lives.

It's incredibly lonely when you're "right" all the time.

We don't have to be this way. Let's not love the quarrels. We don't have to build walls to protect our egos. We don't have to be right and lonely.

We can keep our mouths shut on those things where it really doesn't matter. Living at peace with people is more important than being right.

We can look at those opportunities when we must correct others as a chance to help them to look as good as they can for the Lord.

We can receive correction in humility when we're wrong (and we will be!).

Don't be right and lonely. Be peaceful and blessed while you are speaking peace and blessing.

18 – A LITTLE BIT OF KNOWLEDGE (PROVERBS 18:2)

"Knowing just a little bit can be dangerous."

I've heard this most of my life from my parents. It was a warning to me not to let a little bit of knowledge become more important to me than pursuing wisdom.

It's a strange thing with us as humans: we learn just a little bit and then proceed to carry off as if we're suddenly experts. Not only are we most certainly *not* experts with a little bit of knowledge, but we can also be dangerous to those without *any* knowledge in that area.

We'll come across with the confidence of an expert when we are barely two steps ahead of the novice. That's dangerous.

This is the warning of **Proverbs 18:2**:

Fools find no pleasure in understanding
but delight in airing their own opinions.

Biblically speaking, a fool is not only someone who is ignorant (without knowledge), but someone who also has some level of moral deficiency. While they may not be the worst human ever to walk the

Earth, they usually are as spiritually ignorant as they are intellectually ignorant.

This Proverb tells us the fool has so much pride they think they know it all. There's nothing more they can learn because they are already experts.

Several months ago, I was perusing Facebook and came across an article making my eyes roll. Worse, the person sharing it prefaced the article with their inflammatory comments about how bad this church was with its "worldly approach to ministry."

This person is not a pastor. This person is not a ministry leader. This person attends church services several times a month, but they can't stand their church. With hardly any Biblical training they didn't receive through reading articles like this one on the Internet, the only skills this person brought to the equation was their perceived excellence of opinion.

Christians, we should be afraid of those whose minds are closed while their mouths are open.

They are not helping the cause of Christ.

They're not helping anybody but themselves.

Don't turn off your discernment just because someone claims to be giving you useful information—me included! Scripture encourages us to do our work. Hold everything against the grid of Scripture.

Moreover, hold what "the fool" says against the standard of their own lives. The Lord transforms us by His Word, and when we share it, it comes from the overflow of our lives. Otherwise, it's just regurgitation of someone else's thoughts.

Find pleasure today in basking in the Lord's wisdom. Open your mind and heart to Him. Learn more and speak less. For the wise, their lives demonstrate their wisdom. For the fools...well...they'll have to tell you how wise they are.

19 – DON'T SWING! (PROVERBS 19:11)

"Don't swing at pitches in the dirt."

My dad must have said this to me over and over again as he was teaching me to swing a bat. That and "keep your eye on the ball." I needed both pieces of advice.

It's easy to get up to your turn at bat and swing at anything coming remotely close to the plate. After all, you're there to hit the ball, and you can't hit it if you don't swing, right? You have (perhaps) even odds of hitting the ball if you're swinging, but you're guaranteed 0% chance of hitting the ball when the bat rests on your shoulder. So most of us get programmed to swing, swing, swing.

But when the ball is coming at your feet, you have milliseconds to decide if you're going to try to hit it out of the dirt (more akin to golf) or let it go. The advice my dad always gave me? Don't swing at pitches in the dirt. You can't hit them, and even if you did, the ball is not going anywhere but a foot or two away from you. It's a "ball" (as opposed to a "strike"); let it go.

Not only is this a good piece of advice if you're playing baseball, but it's also excellent advice for life as well. How many times do we come across situations where someone throws a "pitch in the dirt" and we're faced with milliseconds to decide if we're going to swing at this

43

very low pitch or let it go.

Here's the advice of **Proverbs 19:11**:

A person's wisdom yields patience;
it is to one's glory to overlook an offense.

There are two key points we need to see, and they are bound in two words, *"wisdom"* and *"glory."*

The word *"wisdom"* can be understood as "discretion". In other words, our discretion yields patience. And why is that? Why can't we swing at every pitch in the dirt and defend ourselves? If the person is wrong in their accusation, why can't we address it each and every time?

Sometimes you do. But the reality is—read this slowly—you can't address it every time. You'll do nothing but waste a lot of time defending yourself. Your discretion yields patience. With wisdom (from God), you'll know when you need to address it. Most of the time, however, you'll need to let it go. After all, *"Discretion will protect you, and understanding will guard you"* (**Proverbs 2:11**).

Then there's the word *"glory"*. The Hebrew word refers to a quality of being magnificent or splendid. Taken in context, we can gather that we are better people when we *"overlook an offense."* Note: it **IS** an offense; not just our imagination. With this kind of "glory," we can live lives clothed *"with compassion, kindness, humility, gentleness and patience"* (**Colossians 3:12b**).

Bottom line: this jewel of wisdom speaks to our Christ-empowered ability to make HUGE allowances for the frailty and sinfulness of humanity. With the Lord's help, we can allow most of the pitches in the dirt to pass us by and not allow ourselves to wallow in the mud.

So whatever you do, *"Don't swing at pitches in the dirt!"*.

20 – DARK HAIR AND GRAY HAIR
(PROVERBS 20:29)

Defy your age!

Watch TV for more than a few minutes (without fast forwarding through the commercials because you've DVR'd it) and you'll see a commercial heralding some cream, lotion, exercise, device, or apparatus as the next "fountain of youth."

I'm "that guy" who always asks "why?" and "what's the endgame?". And when I turn that lens towards these commercials, the message it sends is pretty simple—I bet you get the message even if you're not on the OCD side of analyzing messages—young is good and old is bad. Is that true?

If you're a Christian as most of my readers are, then we have another angle to see that is something beyond the cultural one. We have to ask what the Bible thinks of these messages. Here's where the Bible has more to say on the subject. And it's not what you think.

We read in **Proverbs 20:29**:

The glory of young men is their strength,
gray hair the splendor of the old.

Culture tells us defying our age and looking "Forever 21" is the preferred state to be in. Religious folks tell us "old is better." The Biblical truth: neither is condemned. Both are praised.

But it's still not that simple. This Proverb is presented as a paired statement. In other words, these are complementary ideas. They need each other to find fulfillment. Read that slowly: they need each other to find fulfillment.

From the young, we gain drive, strength, and the relentless press against the word "impossible." From the old, we gain wisdom, perspective, and counsel.

In His wisdom, the Lord has provided an excellent treasure chest in our lives in multiple generations. What a loss to us if we fail to take advantage of these resources. The young are apt to rely on sheer exercise of power and stamina while the older have learned restraint and patience. Both are needed.

And nowhere do we get more sideways on this than in the church. We believe that only by separating every generation from the others can we adequately meet their "needs." Scripture, it seems, disagrees.

If you place yourself in the "young" category, know the great advantage you bring to the table. If you place yourself in the "old" category, know the great advantage you bring to the table. My advice? Find each other. Learn from each other. Show the world how Christians value the entire spectrum of human life, from the cradle to the grave.

And in finding each other and depending on cross-generational bonds, we all can defy our age.

21 – WORKING TOO FAST (PROVERBS 21:5)

"Haste Makes Waste"

You ever been told that? If you move too fast you're not working efficiently anymore; you're just slopping through it.

I remember hearing this in fifth grade. I did not want to do my work in class, and so I hurried through the assignment so I could get back to what I wanted to do: draw.

I'm reasonably certain the quality of my work was shoddy because when I took it to the teacher—triumphant in my being the first to finish—she looked at me and said, *"Joel, haste makes waste."* She handed it back to me and made me do it again.

King Solomon of Israel—the most likely source of this English idiom—would have said it this way to me:

The plans of the diligent lead to profit
as surely as haste leads to poverty.
Proverbs 21:5

Shortcuts in life are rarely beneficial. I'm not saying they're *never* beneficial, but they are rare. Profit of any kind is not found in cutting corners, short-changing the process, or riding roughshod through the task. That's *"haste"*.

It's a nice way of describing another form of laziness. Diligence is hard; sloppy is (much) easier.

Slow and steady really does win the race. *"Plans of the diligent"* are profitable. Those who are careful to *"measure twice and cut once"* prove the most effective.

Planning your work and working your plan is not just a cute expression; it's Biblical. It's wise.

Think of our spiritual growth. If that is our profit, then we will not get there by hastily hurrying the process. How can we cut corners spiritually? One way is faking it.

If you've been a Christian for a few years, you know how to "God talk". Just throw in a few "praying", "blessed", and "God is good!" and you've got the beginning of top-notch Christianese. Some of your Christian friends will be impressed.

But *"haste leads to poverty."* In the case of our spiritual growth, this means poverty of our spirits. We'll fake it well, but when the storms of life hit, our spiritual bank will have nothing to draw from, and we'll fall prey to our own shortcut.

Instead, dear one in Jesus, plan the diligence you'll need to prosper spiritually (or any other way!). Plan your time with Jesus—schedule it out. Commit to it for at least six weeks to help it become a habit. Dig in and pay the dues it takes to grow.

Life with Jesus is like a muscle: it's got to be exercised.

My fifth-grade teacher may or may not have been trying to teach me about spiritual growth (probably not), but the Word of the Lord provides us wisdom in all areas of our lives.

Haste makes waste, and diligence just makes more sense.

22 – GET RICH—REALLY RICH
(PROVERBS 22:1)

You could soon find yourself not needing to leave your house to make money!

It certainly got my attention as a college student: I could sit in my dorm room, make a few phone calls, maybe do a little showing of products and—poof!—I'd be a millionaire before I even graduated. Well, I'm not a millionaire and I'm a long way after that graduation.

If you want to get someone's attention really quickly, start talking about money. From Fox Business to CNBC, we Americans are very interested in how to get money, how to spend money, and how to repeat the process so we get more to spend more. Granted, it's not everybody, but it certainly seems to fit.

But did you know there's a type of wealth more fragile, but infinitely more valuable? It is THE key to your relationships, spiritual vitality, and emotional well-being.

To master THIS type of wealth makes you rich…really rich. And it's found in **Proverbs 22:1**.

A good name is more desirable than great riches;
to be esteemed is better than silver or gold.

Now I know what some of you might be thinking: *"Hey! You tricked me! My reputation has nothing to do with me being rich!"*

Oh, beloved of the Father, how mistaken you are.

Your name is what you have control over. You can't change what comes and goes into your bank account sometimes. You can't change what property values do. You can't change what your employer might do to your 401K or what the insurance companies do to your rates. But you can, however, seek the great riches of a good name.

A good name makes you rich. To be a person whom others know is a person of dignity, respect, and honor is worth more than money. You can always make more money, but your reputation—once spent—proves very, very (very, very) difficult to rebuild and reclaim.

It pays to be cautious with the wealth of your good name. Perhaps this is why we are encouraged to *"reject every kind of evil"* (**1 Thessalonians 5:22**).

So today, seek to be a person of character, competence, and constancy. Be the one taking the high road. As a follower of Christ, you are a son or daughter of the King. And this King Whose Name you bear has the Name above all names and gives us His Name. This Name testifies to the world of the change He's made in our lives.

With our good name, empowered by Him, we can learn the secret of being rich…really rich.

23 – FOCUS! (PROVERBS 23:17-18)

"Focus!"

When our older child was four years old, she was fairly typical. She can be walking along and suddenly run into something—like a door or a person—and often I find myself telling her, "Dani, focus!" She's in another world at those moments: a world of her toys, snacks, and friends.

I hope that my call to "look out" will begin to instill the very practical skill of paying attention.

I'll have to get back to you on if it works.

Just like I try to do this for my child, our heavenly Father fills His "manual for living"—AKA, the Bible—with instructions declaring, "focus!" Sometimes it works...other times we're too busy in our own little worlds and run into things.

Proverbs 23:17-18 is one such place in the Bible and gives us wise advice:

Do not let your heart envy sinners,
but always be zealous for the fear of the Lord.
There is surely a future hope for you,
and your hope will not be cut off.

The words translated as *"envy"* and *"zealous"* come from the same root word in Hebrew and could be understood as "jealous." So the counsel of Scripture here is pretty straightforward: *don't be jealous of sinners but be jealous for the Lord. There's a future in being jealous for the Lord, and that future pays off.*

But it's not in understanding where we struggle with this Proverb, is it? It's in doing it.

The world is attractive and alluring. It calls to us by appealing to the very desires in us that would destroy our lives. It attempts to press us into the mold of what those without Christ and without hope live in. Logically, it makes no sense but spiritually…we better be paying attention.

We lose focus. We look down. We spend our energy pursuing what the world tells us we're supposed to have: money, education, security, a house, cars, and stuff we don't need for problems we don't really have. The desire is real. The greed is real. The danger is real.

And we as Christians can sometimes only see it after we've run aground and we're beginning to capsize.

Why?

Because we lose focus. At least, we lose focus on what's truly (read: eternally!) important and focus on things that are only valuable because humans have determined that they are.

The spiritual advice provided in this Proverb also forms a "how-to" for it as well: look up (verse 17) and look ahead (verse 18). Let me paraphrase a C.S. Lewis quote: the most effective Christians in this life are the ones focused on the next.

Friends in Christ, we need to cultivate our uplook to improve our outlook.

Focus! Focus! Focus!

24 – WEEDS OF THE HEART
(PROVERBS 24:30-34)

"Weeds in the front means sloppiness inside."

Years ago, I heard this tidbit of business wisdom. If you see weeds in the front, it means there's sloppiness inside. In other words, if a company didn't bother to trim up the weeds in their front yard (or at their storefront), then there must not be anything good going on inside.

It boils down to the idea that if they don't care about their business, then we shouldn't expect too much from them either.

Perhaps this tidbit was originally based on the wisdom of Solomon from Proverbs because we read in **Proverbs 24:30-34**:

I went past the field of a sluggard,
past the vineyard of someone who has no sense;
thorns had come up everywhere,
the ground was covered with weeds,
and the stone wall was in ruins.
I applied my heart to what I observed
and learned a lesson from what I saw:
A little sleep, a little slumber,

a little folding of the hands to rest—
and poverty will come on you like a thief
and scarcity like an armed man.

The king describes walking past a field maintained by a lazy person without the sense to realize the message they are sending. He noticed thorns, weeds, and the disrepair of the garden walls. This disregard for caring for one's property conveyed an undeniable message to King Solomon.

But as he chewed on this visual, the Great Teacher of Israel saw another meaning to this weed-infested, dilapidated property: a metaphor for our lives.

Laziness, or sloth, takes many forms—none of them good. It causes us to push off what should be done now and temps us to quietly sit and relax when there's work to be done.

The Bible is not telling us rest is bad, but rest is a result of work. We rest because we have accomplished something needing resting from!

When we consider the garden of our lives, what does it look like? Are there thorns of half-informed opinions and weeds of bitterness? Are the boundaries of our hearts lying in ruins?

How's your garden?

Scripture warns us of the consequences of ignoring our gardens: our lives will be marked by emotional (and probably literal) poverty and scarcity. We'll always be frazzled and living from one catastrophe to another.

The weeds of our lives are seen by everyone, and it conveys something about the value of what's inside. Dear Christian, pull out the rake of Bible study. With this, get the shovel of prayer, the hoe of confession, and the mortar of praise.

Let's get to work on cleaning up the gardens of our hearts and show the world the transforming power of the Gospel in our lives.

25 – GRACE SHAKERS (PROVERBS 25:21-22)

I like autumn...I blame my wife.

Until Patty came into my life, I didn't much care about the transition between summer and winter. It was merely a transition for me—not a *real* season. But my wife changed all that for me.

The cool winds of autumn blowing through our trees and cooling the air (at least here in California!) provide not only a break from the heat but also a season full of its own, unique expressions.

It's a great time to settle in and appreciate the warmth of pumpkin-flavored drinks and foods. Cinnamon, ginger, brown sugar...they all smell like autumn to me. Autumn is now my second favorite time of year (Winter still has my heart!).

Think about it: what makes the flavors of this time of year so special? Because we only use them in this combination and this concentration during this season. And what a great time to re-infuse our lives with seasonings of grace, too.

Proverbs 25:21-22 instructs...

If your enemy is hungry, give him food to eat;
if he is thirsty, give him water to drink.

In doing this, you will heap burning coals on his head,
and the Lord will reward you.

For the longest time, I thought this was a type of revenge on those who mistreat us. After all, you could burn their heads by being nice to them. What sweet revenge, right? Unfortunately for my bruised ego, it isn't. Instead, this is sprinkling the seasoning of grace onto someone who needs it most.

Anyone can love someone who loves him or her. Anyone can provide wonderful aromas of affection on someone who sings their praises. But what about the one who doesn't like you and most definitely does NOT sing your praises? How's your grace shaker now?

Jesus told us to liberally sprinkle grace and love our enemies. He reminded us that His kids do not slap someone back because they've slapped us. In the place of the rotten stench of hatred, we cover our enemies with "grace gravy" (**Matthew 5:43-48**).

When autumn comes upon us, take a deep breath and enjoy the unique smells of the delicious (and high calorie) food of this season.

Think about how you can be that sweet aroma to those who dislike, disdain, and distract you.

Be a grace shaker on them—not out of revenge, but out of a genuine love that Jesus has shown you.

Shake away!

26 – DOG'S EARS AND THANKSGIVING MEALS (PROVERBS 26:17)

Thanksgiving is kinda funny.

Occurring on the fourth Thursday in November, this is a day handed to us by Americans who have gone before. It's the day we pause to give God thanks for all we have before we rush out and wait to buy more stuff we want on "Black Friday."

Was that harsh? Too fast—too abrupt? Is that jumping too personal, too quickly?

It certainly brings up a point we need to remember everyday— whether it's the fourth Thursday of November or not. And that point is the "good word" found in **Proverbs 26:17**:

> *Like one who grabs a stray dog by the ears*
> *is someone who rushes into a quarrel not their own.*

Grabbing a stray dog by the ears is a certain way to inflict pain on everyone involved—and yes, this means you, too. We read that first part of that Proverb and think how dumb it would be to find a wild, hungry, stray dog and grab their ears.

But then we go sticking our noses where they don't belong.

Relationships—especially family relationships—can be complicated. Holidays are complicated. Thanksgiving especially.

We typically surround ourselves with family that we probably don't normally spend a whole lot of time with and prepare feasts costing exorbitant amounts of money and hope the attenders survive the holiday.

No family is perfect and few families are absolutely dreadful, but most families have specific subjects that are best left out of our holiday festivities.

My family contains several theological nerds—I'm one of them. And "they" say there are two things you shouldn't discuss: politics and religion. We discuss both. :-)

But we all know there are certain things we don't need to get into unless we want a family feud on our hands. So how dumb would I be to throw one of those "atomic bombs" into the mix in the middle of a family gathering?

Pretty dumb.

And that's the point of the Proverb: don't rush into fights that aren't yours. In the case of family get-togethers, it would mean don't rush into fights that aren't yours to fight right now. Keep the peace. Don't "grab a dog's ears" unless you want to get bitten.

This doesn't mean you are a doormat. It means you're wise and focus on all you have to be thankful for. Which—we all know—is a lot.

Perhaps it might help you to think through and commit to paper those things you do NOT need to bring up at family gatherings— mainly the big ones. Not because they don't ever need to be addressed, but it would cause needless strife when the group can't deal with it.

Instead of causing a fight by grabbing a dog by its ears, be thankful for all you have in your life. Mind your business and thank the Lord for the gift of eternal life.

27 – KISSES AND PUNCHES
(PROVERBS 27:5-6)

"You're my brother in Christ, and I need to tell you this for your own good."

Taken in isolation, that sentence is enough to elicit some strong reactions. Anger would logically be one. A big eye roll would reasonably be another. Crying might even be part of it.

It all depends on the source, right?

There are plenty of people who will try to speak into your life that have no business doing so. They struggle with logs in their eye but see clearly to see the specks of dust in yours (cf. **Matthew 7:3-5**).

And I've had people tell me things predicated by this sentence.

But the specific circumstance I'm recalling was very different. This was (and still is!) a dear brother in Christ. He truly is like a brother to me. I value his counsel, wisdom, and spiritual insight. He holds me accountable for keeping my family before ministry.

My marriage and fatherhood are better because of him.

However, what followed these words was a stern correction about a blind spot in my life that he *knew* was holding me back from my destiny as a pastor. He believed in me and saw I was holding myself back.

And he held no punches in telling me so that morning in Starbucks.

And I'm so very grateful for him. He embodies **Proverbs 27:5-6**:

Better is open rebuke
than hidden love.
Wounds from a friend can be trusted,
but an enemy multiplies kisses.

When love is hidden, it's like no love at all. If you're in a dating or marriage relationship, you can understand this: if your affections are hidden, you'll suck the joy and love right out of that relationship.

Paralleling verse five is verse six giving us an illustration. A friend willing to give us a good "punch" is more valuable than anything else.

People who don't truly love you will tell you what you want to hear. Whether it's fear, not caring, anger, or some other motivation, these "enemies" will let us blindly destroy ourselves by never taking the risk to tell us the truth about ourselves.

How do we put these Proverbs into our wisdom repertoire?

First, develop that relationship with someone where you can be honest with them because you love them and want the best for them— like my friend is for me. Tell them the truth. If they're a jerk, they need to know that. You may be the only person they will even hear that from.

Second, receive the *"wounds of a friend"* well. Get over your ego and know they are offering correction *because* they love you. They want the best for you. In no way am I telling you to receive every random piece of criticism from every hypocrite around you. But I am saying, consider the critique of a friend as a gift from God.

63

By developing these types of relationships, we will continue on our journey to becoming people who make a real difference in the world. We will be used by our Lord to bless others and live out our purpose in Jesus.

28 – UNDERSTANDING "RIGHT" (PROVERBS 28:5)

"You can't blame the world for acting like 'the world' because they don't know any better."

I don't know where I first heard it, but I've said it so many times that it feels like my own. We Christians can do funny things (well, actually, they are infuriating things…). We can expect the world to act like us to the point where we forget that "the world" needs more Jesus and less legalism.

I speak this saying either to myself or to other Christians as a reminder that the sinfulness we see in our culture and society is a product of Genesis 3. It is the fall of humanity that introduced the brokenness all around us, and it's working itself out to the only logical conclusion sin has: death.

No, it's not a popular message, but when considering an expression like that, it bears deep thought. And it comes from the most logical place: the Bible. In **Proverbs 28:5** we read…

Evildoers do not understand what is right,
but those who seek the Lord understand it fully.

For so long, Western Christianity and Western politics shared an unusual relationship. It was not this way for the early church. Back in the late first century, into the second century, and at various points along the way, Christians were strikingly different from those around them. We were truly a counter-cultural movement.

The founders of our nation spoke openly and freely about their Christian faith and expressed the sentiment that one could not call themselves an American if they could not call themselves a Christian.

Today, calling oneself a Christian and living by the code that confession demands is a quick way to lose votes and possibly even entire elections (depending on what part of the country you're in).

So when someone is shocked by the immorality that is accepted as normative or when we hear of one more judge preventing Christians from exercising their religion, it verifies the words of **Proverbs 28:5**: justice is impossible without God.

When we read the first five books of the Old Testament, collectively called the Torah, we quickly see how concerned the Lord is with justice. Yet we as Christians can lose the Biblical concept of justice and understanding what is "right" because we have so combined our nationality with our faith that everything becomes a political quagmire.

But when we seek the Lord and His righteousness, we start to perceive what justice really is. We become righteously indignant over the things that would displease our Heavenly Father. We begin to understand where the battles are that need our opinion and voice.

Yes, dear Christian, because the Gospel has changed us, we change our world.

We vote differently.
We spend differently.
We feel differently.
We become "salt and light" to our world (cf. **Matthew 5:13-14**).

As the late Robert Webber wrote, the ultimate question for a Christian living in America to ask is *not* "How is America?" but "How is the church?" (*Ancient-Future Faith: Rethinking Evangelicalism for a Postmodern World*, 168).

Seek the Lord, understand His definition of justice fully, and be the hands and feet of our Creator to your world.

29 – IT'S A TRAP! (PROVERBS 29:25)

"How many in here admit to being 'people pleasers'?"

My hand went up halfway. After all, there were many in my church at which I was Lead Pastor who would say I wasn't a people pleaser. I knew I struggled with it.

The facilitator of this "Marriage and Ministry Seminar" was quick to call me down, "You KNOW you are! That's why you feel like you're supposed to raise your hand, but you're not sure if you should." He laughed. I laughed. My friend with me laughed.

The point of this exercise was to prove that all pastors are people pleasers. After all, "people" is what we "do". Without people, you can't be a pastor. And what pastor doesn't care one iota if his people are happy?

It got me thinking.

And it should get you thinking too.

How many of us are people pleasers? How many of us decide what to do based on who will be offended rather than on what needs to be done?

Really.

Proverbs 29:25 challenges…

Fear of man will prove to be a snare,
but whoever trusts in the Lord is kept safe.

At the root of our people pleasing is one thing: fear. And if we're really, really honest: it's more of a fear of our own rejection than hurting someone else's feelings.

People can get over hurt feelings but what about us…can we?

Part of being a leader in any way, shape, or form is the ability to make the "tough calls". In my universe, it may mean saying "no" to a great ministry-related opportunity because it lays outside of our core values.

Or it could be "pulling the plug" on a ministry that's no longer doing what it set out to do.

That's the calling of leadership: making the tough calls to keep the mission going.

But I'd be lying if I didn't say I didn't factor in the human equation. I want people to like me, and I know they won't like me (even if it's only for a little bit) once I make those "tough calls."

What if that fear ensnares me to the point where I'm crippled to inaction?

What if you feel that tugging in your heart to talk to that friend about Jesus or about how they're living? Do you risk it? What if they're offended? Can you take the rejection?

If you walk too far down that path, you'll be ensnared to inaction.

Alternatively, trusting the Lord protects us from these snares. Rest assured, those people-pleasing tendencies will still pop up from time to time, but when they do, you'll know that's a trap.

When we've already determined Who we will follow, walking the path is much easier.

"No one who puts a hand to the plow and looks back," Jesus said, *"is fit for service in the kingdom of God"* (**Luke 9:62**).

Trust in where the Lord is calling you to go. Trust in who the Lord is calling you to be. Trust in why He has you walking in the first place. Trade the trap of people pleasing for Jesus-pleasing.

"His master replied, 'Well done, good and faithful servant! You have been faithful with a few things; I will put you in charge of many things. Come and share your master's happiness!'" (Jesus in **Matthew 25:21**).

30 – HAND OVER MOUTH INSTEAD OF FOOT IN MOUTH (PROVERBS 30:32-33)

I could not believe he said that to me.

I was—what's a nice word?—incensed. Beside myself. Seeing red. Mad as a hornet.

The infraction was legitimate: this fellow pastor disrespected me in front of others with a heartless statement. He wasn't backing down. My personality type doesn't back down either.

It was a standoff.

And as I took a breath to respond, the Lord reminded me of the words of a friend. These words were an application of **Proverbs 30:32-33**:

If you play the fool and exalt yourself,
or if you plan evil,
clap your hand over your mouth!
For as churning cream produces butter,
and as twisting the nose produces blood,
so stirring up anger produces strife.

It's easy to look back and think *"I shouldn't have done that."* Hindsight, after all, is 20/20. But what if we cultivated the Lord's mind in us to the point where we saw it coming? Imagine the pain we'd avoid if we shut down our egos <u>before</u> we hurt people.

Is it possible?

This Proverb indicates it is.

If you are putting yourself in a position of pride, *"clap your hand over your mouth!"* it warns. If we don't stop ourselves before proceeding into the result of our own foolishness, our *"stirring up anger"* will only produce *"strife"*.

In other words: pot stirrers only get burned by their own brew.

Good advice, huh? You can write that one down. ☺

But what does it take to get there?

The two-part answer is in the Proverb itself.

1. Recognize your ability to be unwise (*"play the fool"*) occasionally.
2. Acknowledge your heart is naturally drawn to *"plan evil"*.

The summary of those two points is merely this: apart from Jesus, our hearts will mislead us.

The advice my friend gave me years ago that kept me from laying into that guy on that day was this: *"Act in the opposite spirit."*

When you want to yell in anger, act in the opposite spirit.

When you want to knock the daylights out of that person, act in the opposite spirit.

When you want to use what you know against someone else, act in the opposite spirit.

When you want to *"plan evil"*, *"clap your hand over your mouth."* The alternative is simply not worth defacing your reputation in Christ over.

31 – STAND UP (PROVERBS 31:8-9)

"Leave him alone!"

I remember these words leaving my lips when I saw a smaller boy getting picked on by children in my grade. I knew this boy would have been clobbered if someone didn't stand up for him and I was always taught to defend those who need defending.

So, I threw it out there to these boys: "leave him alone!"

Unbelievably, they did leave him alone, and this boy remained a friend throughout elementary school.

Even children recognize those with power must care for those without it. It doesn't change as we age as **Proverbs 31:8-9** reminds us:

Speak up for those who cannot speak for themselves,
for the rights of all who are destitute.
Speak up and judge fairly;
defend the rights of the poor and needy.

The instructions from the King to his son were clear: defend the defenseless. And this should have been the mandate of the King of Israel. After all, the earthly king represented the Heavenly King to the people.

Our Lord is very concerned about the needs of those who don't have as much as others. Often, the Lord uses those who have something to give to those who have less.

As a holy nation (cf. **1 Peter 2:9**), we as Christians are not removed from this obligation. Nowadays, it's noble and popular to care for the poor. Dare I say: it's glamorous now. Social Media helps us take selfies while we serve the homeless and hungry and post pictures of our international mission trips that only the wealthiest nations on Earth could mount.

It's not that posting pictures is a bad thing. It's just often done for the wrong reason.

Without Jesus in our lives and as our motivating force, we are caring for others out of selfish motives. We care for those who will bring us the most credit instead of those actually needing the most help.

In other words: we are doing it because of what it does for us instead of what it does for them.

Here's why: Jesus was concerned for the orphans and widows. These represented the parts of society that were easiest to forget. In a sense, they were a burden to everyone else. Jesus was showing us to be His hands and feet and bless those people with His love and provision.

Who are those who need the most help today? Here are a few: the elderly, the mentally challenged, and the unborn.

Therefore we *"speak up for those who cannot speak for themselves."* They have no power, and we have some. I know there are some of you who might disagree with this, but the greatest example of those who cannot speak for themselves are the unborn.

Abortion is a scourge on our nation, and the fact that it still exists reminds us as Christians that we have not opened our mouths for those *"who cannot speak for themselves."*

We defend the defenseless not because it's easy, simple, friendly, fun, or popular. Instead, we do it because we have been brought from darkness into light by the lavish grace of God the Father through His Son, Jesus Christ.

Get out there, dear Christian! We need you. Choose God's causes, put on your spiritual armor, and stand up. The mission of God is waiting.

32 – WHAT'S NEXT

You made it!

After a full month in the Proverbs, you've done something worth celebrating! You didn't just finish a book, you've spent time with the Lord's wisdom from His Word.

As we continue growing in our transformed life in Jesus, the Holy Spirit's encouragement to us is to "take the next step."

Where do you go from here?

Might I suggest taking some S.I.P.S.?

S.I.P.S. is a method I use for my personal worship time with the Lord. Maybe it can help you too.

S – Sing. Music is such a powerful way to express our adoration of the Lord. Singing not only helps us feel better, but it also has a way of engaging mind, emotion, and spirit. Get your favorite worship music, put it on, and sing along.

I – Investigate. This is your Bible reading and exploration. I'm biased towards the wisdom of the Proverbs (by now, you've realized that!). My suggestion is reading a chapter of the Proverbs daily. It's not a stopping point, but it's a start.

P – Pray. There are a lot of resources guiding this time. Since I'm giving acrostics, here's one to help with prayer: A.C.T.S. Adoration, Confession, Thanksgiving, and Supplication (a big, fancy word for "prayer requests").

S – Stay. Staying is the hardest for most of us, but the Holy Spirit rarely shouts. His voice can be hidden by our distraction. Staying is the time after we say "amen" and we just wait. We slow ourselves. We calm down. We listen. We…wait. Some call this "marinating in His presence."

Whether you take some S.I.P.S. or use some other method, the "secret sauce" is to take the next step. My prayer for you is that you continue to *"grow in the grace and knowledge of our Lord and Savior Jesus Christ"* (**1 Peter 3:18**).

ABOUT THE AUTHOR

Child of God. Husband. Dad. Pastor.

This summarizes who Joel Dorman is—in that order. Joel is married to Patty, and they have two children. He is the Lead Pastor of First Baptist Church of Merced.

Joel specializes in leadership and strategic development of church leaders for the advance of the Gospel. When he's not writing a message, leading his church or coaching others, Joel enjoys lots of family time, outdoor cooking, watching movies, and enjoying music. He is also a self-proclaimed "Christmas elf."

He holds a Master of Divinity from Liberty Baptist Theological Seminary and a Doctor of Ministry From Trinity Evangelical Divinity School.

You can reach him for leadership coaching (individual or staff) through www.lifemeetstheology.com.

Made in the USA
Las Vegas, NV
13 February 2021